Consider the Ant

Winter is Coming – Be Prepared

ARCHIE L. MCINNIS, II

Printed in the United States of America First Printing, 2026
ISBN: 979-8-234-.02612-5

Full Effect Gospel Ministries, Inc.
Brooklyn, NY

DEDICATION

To every believer navigating changing seasons,
To those who have endured winters they did not expect,
And to those whom God is awakening before the next one comes…

CONTENTS

INTRODUCTION

A small teacher with a serious message…

God often hides His greatest lessons in the smallest places. In Proverbs, He does not summon us to a king, a priest, or a prophet. He sends us to an ant. No platform. No title. No applause. Just wisdom in motion.

"Go to the ant, thou sluggard; consider her ways, and be wise."

This is not poetry for entertainment. It is instruction for survival. God is warning His people that seasons change, opportunity closes, and unprepared living produces unnecessary hardship. Winter is not a punishment; it is a certainty. Wisdom prepares before conditions shift.

This book is not written to condemn the sluggard, but to awaken the wise who have been drifting into delay, comfort, and complacency. The ant teaches us how to live ready in uncertain times.

The wisdom of God often whispers before it warns.
In Scripture, God does not shout through thunder. He points us to an ant.

May these pages stir diligence, awaken discipline, and lead you into a life that is ready, rooted, and wise.

Winter is coming, but wisdom prepares.

With pastoral care and prophetic conviction,

Bishop Archie L. McInnis, II

CHAPTER ONE
GO TO THE ANT

Wisdom begins with humility. Before God instructs, He commands us to observe. "Consider her ways," He says. That word consider means to look closely, to study patterns, to reflect deeply.

The ant does not talk; she moves. She does not explain; she prepares. Her wisdom is not loud, but it is lasting.

Many people want divine direction without divine observation. They pray for answers while ignoring examples God has already placed in front of them. Wisdom is often learned, not downloaded.

The ant reminds us that consistency outperforms charisma. Small habits, done faithfully, produce great outcomes over time. Those who dismiss small disciplines eventually face big consequences.

If you want wisdom, slow down long enough to observe what works.

CHAPTER TWO
THE SLUGGARD'S BLIND SPOT

"How long wilt thou sleep, O sluggard?"

The sluggard is not always lazy; often, he is delayed. He intends to act, just not now. He plans to prepare, just not yet. He mistakes comfort for rest and avoidance for patience.

Delay feels harmless until the season changes. What could have been done easily now becomes difficult later. The sluggard's blind spot is believing time will always cooperate.

Every season of postponement creates pressure in another season.

Financial delays become emergencies.

Spiritual delays become confusion.

Emotional delays become broken relationships.

God is not angry at the sluggard; He is warning him. Delay is not neutral; it is directional.

CHAPTER THREE
WISDOM WITHOUT A SUPERVISOR

The ant has no overseer, yet she works diligently. This reveals a powerful truth: maturity is self-governed.

Some people only function when supervised, corrected, or pressured. But spiritual maturity means doing what is right even when no one is watching. God looks for people He can trust unattended.

What you do in private determines what God releases in public. Faithfulness unseen builds authority seen. Discipline is not punishment; it is preparation.

The ant does not need reminders. She understands the season.

CHAPTER FOUR
NO OVERSEER, NO EXCUSES

Responsibility is the currency of the Kingdom. The ant does not blame the weather, conditions, or circumstances. She owns her assignment.

Excuses delay growth. Blame transfers responsibility.

Maturity says, "This is mine to manage."

Many people pray for increase but resist responsibility. Yet God never gives increase to those unwilling to manage what they already have.

Ownership is proof of readiness.

The ant teaches us that excuses are unnecessary when purpose is understood.

CHAPTER FIVE
SUMMER IS NOT FOR SLEEPING

Summer represents access, strength, and opportunity. It is the easiest time to prepare, yet many disengage because things feel good.

The ant works hardest when conditions are favorable. She understands that ease is temporary. Opportunity seasons are not for rest—they are for preparation.

Too many people relax when they should be preparing. They rest in summer and panic in winter.

Discernment recognizes seasons. Wisdom responds accordingly.

CHAPTER SIX
GATHERING WHILE IT'S AVAILABLE

Provision without stewardship leads to lack. The ant gathers during harvest because she understands the future.

God provides abundance, but He expects management. Storage is not greed; it is foresight. Saving is not fear; it is wisdom.

Whether it is money, wisdom, relationships, or spiritual strength, what you gather today sustains you tomorrow. Those who consume everything leave nothing for the next season.

Harvest thinking looks ahead.

CHAPTER SEVEN
A LITTLE SLEEP, A LITTLE SLUMBER

Spiritual decline is rarely sudden. It happens in increments—small compromises repeated over time.

"A little" seems harmless, but repetition creates patterns. Complacency dulls urgency. Neglect weakens discernment.

No one plans to drift; they simply stop being intentional.

The ant remains alert. She understands that rest has its place, but discipline has priority.

CHAPTER EIGHT
WHEN COMFORT BECOMES COSTLY

Comfort resists growth. It persuades us to stay where we are when God is calling us forward.

The ant chooses labor over leisure because she values future security over present ease. Comfort avoided now produces stability later.

Avoidance always charges interest. What we refuse to address today will demand attention tomorrow at a higher cost.

Growth always requires discomfort.

CHAPTER NINE
POVERTY THAT TRAVELS

"So shall thy poverty come as one that travelleth."

Poverty here is more than finances. It is readiness. Lack often arrives suddenly, but it forms slowly.

Crisis exposes preparation. When pressure comes, it reveals what was stored or what was neglected.

Prepared people respond; unprepared people panic.

The ant survives winter not because winter is mild, but because preparation was thorough.

CHAPTER TEN
BE PREPARED BEFORE WINTER COMES

Winter represents pressure, uncertainty, and change. It is inevitable, but it is not fatal.

Preparation does not cancel winter; it equips you for it. Wisdom eliminates panic. Foresight secures peace.

The ant enters winter calmly because she planned ahead. Her confidence is not arrogance—it is readiness.

God is calling His people to live ready, not reactive.

CONCLUSION
FROM SLUGGARD TO STEWARD

This book is not about condemnation; it is about correction.

God is raising stewards, not spectators. Prepared believers, not panicked ones.

The ant teaches us that wisdom is quiet, consistent, and future-focused.

Those who listen will not fear changing seasons.

Consider the ant.
Correct the sluggard.
Prepare for winter.
And walk in wisdom.

30 DAY DEVOTIONAL

SCAN HERE TO RECEIVE THE
CONSIDER THE ANT RESOURCE LIST

DAY 1
GO TO THE ANT

Scripture
"Go to the ant, thou sluggard; consider her ways, and be wise:"
— Proverbs 6:6 **(KJV)**

Devotional Reading
God does not begin this instruction with rebuke, but with an invitation. *Go. Consider. Be wise.* Wisdom often begins when we slow down long enough to observe what God is already showing us. The ant has no title, no voice, no authority, yet God says she carries wisdom worth studying. Preparation is not loud. It is consistent, quiet, and intentional.

Prayer
Lord, slow my heart and sharpen my discernment. Teach me to observe before I react and to learn before I suffer. Amen.

Daily Charge
Observe before you speak today.

Journal Prompt
What has God been trying to show me that I've overlooked?

DAY 2
WISDOM IS QUIET

Scripture
"The fear of the LORD is the beginning of knowledge: but fools despise wisdom and instruction."
— Proverbs 1:7 **(KJV)**

Devotional Reading
Wisdom does not demand attention; it waits to be honored. The ant does not announce her preparation—she simply does it. Many miss wisdom because it does not entertain them. Quiet obedience often builds the strongest future.

Prayer
Father, help me honor wisdom even when it is quiet and unseen. Amen.

Daily Charge
Choose consistency over recognition.

Journal Prompt
Where do I need to grow quietly?

DAY 3
HUMILITY OPENS THE DOOR

Scripture
"When pride cometh, then cometh shame: but with the lowly is
wisdom."
— Proverbs 11:2 **(KJV)**

Devotional Reading
Pride resists instruction. Humility receives it. God often teaches us
through places we least expect. The ant teaches us because she is
faithful to her assignment.

Prayer
Lord, remove pride from my heart and make me teachable. Amen.

Daily Charge
Receive correction without defense today.

Journal Prompt
Where do I struggle with humility?

DAY 4
HOW LONG WILL YOU DELAY?

Scripture
"How long wilt thou sleep, O sluggard? when wilt thou arise out of thy sleep?"
— Proverbs 6:9 **(KJV)**

Devotional Reading
Delay feels harmless—until the season changes. God's question is not cruel; it is merciful. *How long?* because time matters. Delayed obedience creates future pressure.

Prayer
Lord, awaken me where I have delayed obedience. Amen.

Daily Charge
Act on one delayed matter today.

Journal Prompt
What have I been putting off?

DAY 5
REST OR AVOIDANCE

Scripture
"Yet a little sleep, a little slumber, a little folding of the hands to sleep:
So shall thy poverty come as one that travelleth; and thy want as an
armed man."
— Proverbs 24:33–34 **(KJV)**

Devotional Reading
Not all rest restores. Some rest avoids responsibility. Wisdom discerns
the difference.

Prayer
God, teach me healthy rest and disciplined living. Amen.

Daily Charge
Complete one avoided task today.

Journal Prompt
Am I resting or avoiding?

DAY 6
TIME IS SPEAKING

Scripture
"To every thing there is a season, and a time to every purpose under the heaven:"
— Ecclesiastes 3:1 **(KJV)**

Devotional Reading
Every season speaks. Wisdom listens. Preparation begins with recognizing where you are.

Prayer
Lord, help me discern my season clearly. Amen.

Daily Charge
Align your actions with your season.

Journal Prompt
What season am I in right now?

DAY 7
NO OVERSEER

Scripture
"Which having no guide, overseer, or ruler,"
— Proverbs 6:7 **(KJV)**

Devotional Reading
Maturity does not require supervision. God trusts those who govern themselves.

Prayer
Father, strengthen my discipline and integrity. Amen.

Daily Charge
Be faithful even when unseen.

Journal Prompt
Who am I when no one is watching?

DAY 8
PRIVATE FAITHFULNESS

Scripture
"He that is faithful in that which is least is faithful also in much…"
— Luke 16:10 **(KJV)**

Devotional Reading
Private habits shape public authority. Faithfulness attracts increase.

Prayer
Lord, strengthen my private walk. Amen.

Daily Charge
Strengthen one private discipline today.

Journal Prompt
What private habit needs attention?

DAY 9
TRUSTED WITH MORE

Scripture (KJV)
"Well done, thou good and faithful servant…"
— Matthew 25:21

Devotional Reading
God entrusts more to those who steward what they already have.

Prayer
God, prepare me for greater responsibility. Amen.

Daily Charge
Be faithful in something small today.

Journal Prompt
What has God already entrusted to me?

DAY 10
NO EXCUSES

Scripture
"Which having no guide, overseer, or ruler,"
— Proverbs 6:7 **(KJV)**

Devotional Reading
Excuses delay growth. Ownership accelerates maturity.

Prayer
Lord, I release excuses and accept responsibility. Amen.

Daily Charge
Own one area fully today.

Journal Prompt
What excuse must I let go of?

DAY 11
OWN YOUR ASSIGNMENT

Scripture
"For every man shall bear his own burden."
— Galatians 6:5 **(KJV)**

Devotional Reading
Responsibility is not punishment—it is purpose.

Prayer
Father, help me steward my assignment faithfully. Amen.

Daily Charge
Do your part without comparison.

Journal Prompt
What is my assignment right now?

DAY 12
FAITHFUL STEWARDS

Scripture
"Moreover it is required in stewards, that a man be found faithful."
— 1 Corinthians 4:2 **(KJV)**

Devotional Reading
God measures faithfulness more than talent.

Prayer
God, make me a faithful steward. Amen.

Daily Charge
Manage what you have wisely today.

Journal Prompt
Where must I grow in faithfulness?

DAY 13
SUMMER IS A GIFT

Scripture
"Provideth her meat in the summer, and gathereth her food in the harvest."
— Proverbs 6:8 **(KJV)**

Devotional Reading
Opportunity is seasonal. Wisdom prepares while access is available.

Prayer
Lord, help me value this season. Amen.

Daily Charge
Prepare while things are stable.

Journal Prompt
What opportunity must I not waste?

DAY 14
DON'T WASTE EASE

Scripture
"Woe to them that are at ease in Zion..."
— Amos 6:1 **(KJV)**

Devotional Reading
Ease can deceive us into inactivity.

Prayer
God, keep me alert even in ease. Amen.

Daily Charge
Prepare instead of disengaging.

Journal Prompt
How has comfort slowed me?

DAY 15
REDEEM THE TIME

Scripture
"Redeeming the time, because the days are evil."
— Ephesians 5:16 **(KJV)**

Devotional Reading
Time is a gift that cannot be reclaimed once wasted.

Prayer
Lord, teach me to redeem my time. Amen.

Daily Charge
Use time intentionally today.

Journal Prompt
Where do I waste time?

DAY 16
GATHER WISELY

Scripture
"And gathereth her food in the harvest."
— Proverbs 6:8 **(KJV)**

Devotional Reading
Gathering requires foresight. What you collect today sustains tomorrow.

Prayer
God, help me gather wisely. Amen.

Daily Charge
Store something beneficial today.

Journal Prompt
What should I be gathering now?

DAY 17
STORAGE IS BIBLICAL

Scripture
"And that food shall be for store to the land against the seven years of famine…"
— Genesis 41:36 **(KJV)**

Devotional Reading
Saving is not fear; it is wisdom.

Prayer
Lord, teach me wise stewardship. Amen.

Daily Charge
Improve one area of stewardship.

Journal Prompt
How do I manage provision?

DAY 18
BUILD RESERVES

Scripture
"There is treasure to be desired and oil in the dwelling of the wise…"
— Proverbs 21:20 **(KJV)**

Devotional Reading
Wise people prepare reserves.

Prayer
God, help me build healthy reserves. Amen.

Daily Charge
Plan for the future today.

Journal Prompt
What reserve do I lack?

DAY 19
A LITTLE ADDS UP

Scripture
"Yet a little sleep, a little slumber…"
— Proverbs 6:10 **(KJV)**

Devotional Reading
Small neglects accumulate into major consequences.

Prayer
Lord, help me correct small compromises. Amen.

Daily Charge
Fix one small issue today.

Journal Prompt
What small habit needs correction?

DAY 20
DRIFT IS REAL

Scripture
"Lest at any time we should let them slip."
— Hebrews 2:1 **(KJV)**

Devotional Reading
Drift happens quietly. Awareness stops it.

Prayer
God, anchor my heart again. Amen.

Daily Charge
Recommit to discipline.

Journal Prompt
Where am I drifting?

DAY 21
STAY ALERT

Scripture (KJV)
"Be sober, be vigilant…"
— 1 Peter 5:8

Devotional Reading
Alertness protects destiny.

Prayer
Lord, keep me spiritually alert. Amen.

Daily Charge
Watch and pray today.

Journal Prompt
How will I remain alert?

DAY 22
COMFORT HAS A COST

Scripture
"So shall thy poverty come as one that travelleth…"
— Proverbs 6:11 **(KJV)**

Devotional Reading
Comfort delays preparation.

Prayer
God, help me choose growth over ease. Amen.

Daily Charge
Step outside comfort today.

Journal Prompt
What comfort limits me?

DAY 23
EMBRACE DISCOMFORT

Scripture
"But let patience have her perfect work…"
— James 1:4 **(KJV)**

Devotional Reading
Growth requires endurance.

Prayer
Lord, strengthen me for growth. Amen.

Daily Charge
Endure instead of escaping.

Journal Prompt
What discomfort must I face?

DAY 24
CHOOSE TRANSFORMATION

Scripture
"Be ye transformed by the renewing of your mind…"
— Romans 12:2 **(KJV)**

Devotional Reading
Transformation is intentional.

Prayer
God, renew my mind daily. Amen.

Daily Charge
Choose change today.

Journal Prompt
What must change in me?

DAY 25
POVERTY THAT TRAVELS

Scripture
"And thy want as an armed man."
— Proverbs 6:11 **(KJV)**

Devotional Reading
Lack often arrives suddenly but forms slowly.

Prayer
Lord, reveal areas of unpreparedness. Amen.

Daily Charge
Strengthen one weak area.

Journal Prompt
Where am I unprepared?

DAY 26
STORMS TEST FOUNDATIONS

Scripture
"He is like a man which built an house… and laid the foundation on a rock."
— Luke 6:48 **(KJV)**

Devotional Reading
Preparation determines endurance.

Prayer
God, strengthen my foundation. Amen.

Daily Charge
Build deeper today.

Journal Prompt
What foundation needs repair?

DAY 27
PEACE THROUGH PREPARATION

Scripture
"Thou wilt keep him in perfect peace…"
— Isaiah 26:3 **(KJV)**

Devotional Reading
Preparation replaces panic with peace.

Prayer
Lord, give me peace through wisdom. Amen.

Daily Charge
Prepare instead of worrying.

Journal Prompt
How does preparation bring peace?

DAY 28
WINTER IS CERTAIN

Scripture
"He that observeth the wind shall not sow…"
— Ecclesiastes 11:4 **(KJV)**

Devotional Reading
Waiting for perfect conditions prevents preparation.

Prayer
God, help me prepare without fear. Amen.

Daily Charge
Plan despite uncertainty.

Journal Prompt
What am I preparing for?

DAY 29
READY FOR EVERY SEASON

Scripture
"And he shall be like a tree planted by the rivers of water…"
— Psalm 1:3 **(KJV)**

Devotional Reading
Prepared lives flourish regardless of season.

Prayer
Lord, establish me firmly. Amen.

Daily Charge
Remain rooted today.

Journal Prompt
What habits must continue?

DAY 30
FROM SLUGGARD TO STEWARD

Scripture
"Go to the ant, thou sluggard; consider her ways, and be wise:"
— Proverbs 6:6 **(KJV)**

Devotional Reading
Wisdom transforms how we live. The ant teaches us diligence,
foresight, and peace.

Prayer
Father, thank You for shaping me through wisdom. I commit to a prepared life.
Amen.

Daily Charge
Live ready—every day.

Final Journal Prompt
What has God changed in me over these 30 days?